Acting Edition

Dramatic Debuts Volume 3

Hesperides
by Gabrielle Hoyt-Disick

Keeping Company
by Michael Bontatibus

So
by Zoë Wilson

Navy Blue Tiles
by Katarzyna Roszczeda

‖SAMUEL FRENCH‖

HESPERIDES Copyright © 2011 by Gabrielle Hoyt-Disick
KEEPING COMPANY Copyright © 2011 by Michael Bontatibus
SO Copyright © 2011 by Zoë Wilson
NAVY BLUE TILES Copyright © 2010, 2011 by Katarzyna Roszczeda
All Rights Reserved

DRAMATIC DEBUTS VOLUME 3 is fully protected under the copyright laws of the United States of America, the British Commonwealth, including Canada, and all member countries of the Berne Convention for the Protection of Literary and Artistic Works, the Universal Copyright Convention, and/or the World Trade Organization conforming to the Agreement on Trade Related Aspects of Intellectual Property Rights. All rights, including professional and amateur stage productions, recitation, lecturing, public reading, motion picture, radio broadcasting, television, online/digital production, and the rights of translation into foreign languages are strictly reserved.

ISBN 978-0-87440-713-6

www.concordtheatricals.com
www.concordtheatricals.co.uk

FOR PRODUCTION INQUIRIES

UNITED STATES AND CANADA
info@concordtheatricals.com
1-866-979-0447

UNITED KINGDOM AND EUROPE
licensing@concordtheatricals.co.uk
020-7054-7200

Each title is subject to availability from Concord Theatricals Corp., depending upon country of performance. Please be aware that *DRAMATIC DEBUTS VOLUME 3* may not be licensed by Concord Theatricals Corp. in your territory. Professional and amateur producers should contact the nearest Concord Theatricals Corp. office or licensing partner to verify availability.

CAUTION: Professional and amateur producers are hereby warned that *DRAMATIC DEBUTS VOLUME 3* is subject to a licensing fee. The purchase, renting, lending or use of this book does not constitute a license to perform this title(s), which license must be obtained from Concord Theatricals Corp. prior to any performance. Performance of this title(s) without a license is a violation of federal law and may subject the producer and/or presenter of such performances to civil penalties. Both amateurs and professionals considering a production are strongly advised to apply to the appropriate agent before starting rehearsals, advertising, or booking a theatre. A licensing fee must be paid whether the title(s) is presented for charity or gain and whether or not admission is charged. Professional/Stock licensing fees are quoted upon application to Concord Theatricals Corp.

This work is published by Samuel French, an imprint of Concord Theatricals Corp.

No one shall make any changes in this title(s) for the purpose of production. No part of this book may be reproduced, stored in a retrieval system, scanned, uploaded, or transmitted in any form, by any means, now known or yet to be invented, including mechanical, electronic, digital, photocopying, recording, videotaping, or otherwise, without the prior written permission of the publisher. No one shall share this title(s), or any part of this title(s), through any social media or file hosting websites.

For all inquiries regarding motion picture, television, online/digital and other media rights, please contact Concord Theatricals Corp.

MUSIC AND THIRD-PARTY MATERIALS USE NOTE

Licensees are solely responsible for obtaining formal written permission from copyright owners to use copyrighted music and/or other copyrighted third-party materials (e.g., artworks, logos) in the performance of this play and are strongly cautioned to do so. If no such permission is obtained by the licensee, then the licensee must use only original music and materials that the licensee owns and controls. Licensees are solely responsible and liable for clearances of all third-party copyrighted materials, including without limitation music, and shall indemnify the copyright owners of the play(s) and their licensing agent, Concord Theatricals Corp., against any costs, expenses, losses and liabilities arising from the use of such copyrighted third-party materials by licensees. For music, please contact the appropriate music licensing authority in your territory for the rights to any incidental music.

IMPORTANT BILLING AND CREDIT REQUIREMENTS

If you have obtained performance rights to this title, please refer to your licensing agreement for important billing and credit requirements.

THE BAKER'S PLAYS HIGH SCHOOL
PLAYWRITING COMPETITION

Baker's Plays has been an advocate for theater in schools for over one hundred years. In the spirit of that commitment, we offer the Baker's High School Playwriting Competition for all High School-aged dramatists interested in the craft of playwriting. It is our hope that this competition will encourage aspiring High School authors to explore the creative possibilities of writing for the stage.

This volume of *Dramatic Debuts* represents the culmination of the 2010 competition. The three plays included in this book display what we at Baker's Plays felt was the strongest understanding of writing for the stage. The plays included in this volume are:

First place
Hesperides by Gabrielle Hoyt-Disick

Second place
Keeping Company by Michael Bontatibus

Third place
So by Zoë Wilson

Fidelity FutureStage® Playwriting Contest Winner
Navy Blue Tiles by Katarzyna Roszczeda

We congratulate these three writers and thank all who participated in the 2010 competition.

For information as to how enter the Baker's Plays High School Playwriting Competition as well as information on past competition winners, visit our website at **BakersPlays.com**.

CONTENTS

Hesperides 7
Keeping Company 25
So 43
Navy Blue Tiles. 59

HESPERIDES

by Gabrielle Hoyt-Disick

PRODUCTION HISTORY

HESPERIDES was directed by Blake Beaver and produced by the Columbia Summer Theater Program in July 2009. Aegle was played by Kathryn Cooperman. Erytheia was played by Rachel Katz. Hespere was played by Caitlin Simpson.

CHARACTER BREAKDOWN

A note about ages–in this play, the characters' actual ages are less important than their ages relative to each other. True, all three sisters act like adolescents, but remember that they're goddesses, not humans, and therefore aren't limited by age as we are.

AEGLE is the oldest sister. This fact weighs on her heavily, and she is constantly trying to prove that she is the leader of the family. However, her obnoxious bossiness is simply a mask that hides her feelings of insecurity and unworthiness.

ERYTHEIA is the middle sister. She copes with her situation by putting up a sarcastic, contrary front, although there are times when she is extremely tender and loving. The most adventurous of the three, she feels trapped and bored by her life, and longs to somehow escape.

HESPERE is the youngest sister. She has been babied by her sisters, and, in many ways, seems much younger than they are. However, she also has powers of insight that the other two lack, and is often frustrated because they refuse to take her seriously.

AUTHOR'S NOTES

The Garden of the Hesperides. A quiet little place at the end of the Earth. The essential feature of this setting is a curtain that can be opened and closed by the inhabitants of the garden. All other scenery should conform to the style of this curtain. If it is, say, light and diaphanous, the scenery should have that same ethereal, exotic effect. If the curtain is black, then perhaps the scenery should be more minimal. Just remember that this is a garden beyond the sunset – by no means should it look real.

The Tree. The Tree causes most, if not all of the action in the play. It resides just behind the place where the two parts of the back curtain comes together so, if a character opens the curtain even slightly, the tree is visible. It is just the height of, or slightly smaller than, the smallest nymph. Without the Apples, it is spindly, lifeless, and unremarkable. When the Apples do hang on the tree, there are three of them. Each Apple dangles from its own string, about one-and-a-half feet long, that is, in turn, attached to one of the branches of the Tree. When the Apples are on the Tree, the Tree should seem to glow, an effect that can be created using a small spotlight. Whenever the Apples are on the tree, Ladon is also wrapped around the tree.

Ladon. Ladon is the serpent charged with protecting the tree. He can be no more than a long, linen scarf, embracing the Tree. When the Apples disappear, he, too, disappears.

The Apples. The Apples themselves are golden. They can be either real apples painted gold, or golden balls. However, if they are not real fruit, then they should not be any bigger than a good-sized apple.

The Sunset Song. The nymphs sing this song every night before the sun sets. It should be beautiful, haunting, and relatively short.

The Hesperides. The nymphs, guardians of the Tree, should fit into their garden, and add to the feeling of unreality. Their costumes do not have to match, but something should connect all of them. It could be the style, or the color, or even the length. These costumes must reflect that the nymphs are sisters, and that they are considered by many to be the physical manifestation of the sunset. The nymphs' are Aegle, Erytheia, and Hespere.

Heracles (more commonly known as Hercules). This mythical hero is represented by clothes on a hanger, which can be carried around by the nymphs, or draped somewhere, depending on the scene. A wooden hanger is preferable. The clothes can conform to our idea of classical "Greece" (a chiton, a toga, a sheet), or can be modern. However, it might be nice for Heracles to have something approximating a lion skin.

The Story. This play is based on the eleventh labor of the ancient Greek hero Heracles. If the director feels that the audience should know this then, by all means, put a small note into the program. However, such a note is not required and, if the director feels that it's unnecessary, then omitting is perfectly fine as well.

ABOUT THE PLAYWRIGHT

Gabrielle Hoyt-Disick wrote *Hesperides* in 2009, but was acting, singing, playing violin, and writing long before then. n addition to winning the Baker's Plays High School Playwriting Contest, she also won second place in the Princeton University Ten-Minute Play Contest, second place in the Union County College Young Playwrights' Competition, and honorable mention in Young Playwrights, Inc. New York City. Her work has been performed at Columbia University, Union County College, and Brown University. Most recently, the Riverdale Country School Parents' Association provided a grant to produce her original satirical musical *Admissions* in the Times Square Arts Center. Special thanks to Mom, Baba, Grampa, and especially Miranda for the inspiration, support, and love.

Scene One

(**AEGLE**, **ERYTHEIA**, *and* **HESPERE** *sit huddled in a circle. The curtains behind them are closed. All three are holding hands tightly, not moving, and not looking at each other.*)

(**HESPERE** *glances at* **AEGLE**.)

(**ERYTHEIA** *glances at* **AEGLE**.)

(**HESPERE** *and* **ERYTHEIA** *look at each other, and then back at* **AEGLE**.)

(**AEGLE** *sees* **HESPERE** *and* **ERYTHEIA** *watching her. As her eyes flick back and forth, her face grows increasingly defensive. She drops her sisters' hands, and determinedly gets up.*)

AEGLE. I am going to go check on the Tree.

(**HESPERE** *makes a small whimpering noise and looks down.*)

(**ERYTHEIA** *stares up at* **AEGLE**.)

ERYTHEIA. *(hopelessly)* Why?

AEGLE. Maybe they've grown back.

HESPERE. *(hysterically)* I'll go, I will, I want to see the Tree, please, and Ladon –

AEGLE. Hespere, I'm the oldest. I go.

(**HESPERE** *subsides, as* **AEGLE** *and* **ERYTHEIA** *exchange looks.*)

(**AEGLE** *walks towards the curtain. It takes her a long time to get there. Both her sisters have averted their eyes.*)

(**AEGLE** *pokes her head through the curtains. Her hands clench, and she quickly draws her head back out. She stands for a moment, her back to the audience, head bowed, before walking back to her sisters.*)

AEGLE. *(cont.)* *(as she sits back down)* Nothing. No change.

*(***HESPERE*** suddenly jumps up, and runs upstage. She violently rips over the curtains, revealing the lifeless Tree. Once she has drawn the curtains back, she stands frozen before the Tree, and then kneels down before it, trembling.)*

*(***AEGLE*** and ***ERYTHEIA*** who have, so far, been staring after ***HESPERE***, amazed, now get up and sit on either side of her. While she stares at the Tree, they both take pains not to look at it.)*

ERYTHEIA. Maybe we should tell someone.

AEGLE. *(glancing nervously at her surroundings)* Tell…who?

ERYTHEIA. *(drily)* You could. You're the oldest.

AEGLE. Erytheia, do you think it's *my* fault?

ERYTHEIA. *(quickly)* I never said that, Aegle, that's not at all what I –

AEGLE. Yes – yes – and those dirty looks you throw me, and you've turned 'Spere against me too, because you don't want to admit –

ERYTHEIA. Where do you get these things from? I mean it, you just pull it out of the air –

*(They begin speaking very quickly at the same time. ***AEGLE*** is more extravagant in terms of gesture and volume, while ***ERYTHEIA*** relies heavily on sarcasm. As they argue, ***HESPERE*** crawls out from between them and wanders around aimlessly, as if looking for someone.)*

AEGLE. You don't want to admit that you had some part in this too, that it's your fault too. I feel sorry for you, I mean it, because you find it impossible to take any responsibility. You just always blame me or 'Spere, and I'm not saying that it's your fault, Erytheia, I just think that you should have the guts to say "It's partly my fault," like I can, but you've never been that brave.

ERYTHEIA. Yes, Aegle, just keep screaming, I know it'll make you feel better. Really, just stand there and scream, and we won't even have to tell anyone, because they'll find out on their own. Because screaming and becoming randomly defensive will definitely make everything better, it'll just take us back in time, and everything will be better.

(The two glare furiously at each other. **AEGLE** *realizes that* **HESPERE** *isn't there. There is a frantic moment, before they see her on stage left.)*

AEGLE. *(turning sharply)* What are you doing?

*(***HESPERE*** drops onto her hands and knees.)*

HESPERE. *(She looks close to tears.)* I thought I saw Ladon.

AEGLE. *(still lashing out)* Hespere, don't be stupid, Ladon's probably –

(She is cut off by **ERYTHEIA***, who has moved swiftly to* **HESPERE***'s side and knelt down.)*

ERYTHEIA. 'Spere, Ladon's a snake. He's probably still scared, and hiding somewhere, that's all. He'll come out when he's ready. You won't find him that way.

*(***ERYTHEIA*** gently helps* **HESPERE** *stand, and they exit left together, with* **ERYTHEIA** *pointedly ignoring* **AEGLE***.)*

*(***AEGLE*** stands alone, staring off towards stage left. She slowly sits down, facing the audience.)*

AEGLE. I wasn't on guard when they were taken. But I did – let him in. And besides that, I was in charge.

I *am* in charge.

We get news, even out here. So I'd heard of Heracles. I just feel so *stupid*. I was so excited, when he came, I got to make the traditional speech, and we showed him the garden…I know I wanted something to happen, sometimes…so that I could do my job for real…but I didn't actually mean…

(She exits.)

Scene Two

(ERYTHEIA and HESPERE walk on. The curtains are closed, and the mood is completely different. HESPERE is blowing bubbles and giggling. ERYTHEIA has a book in her hand. They sprawl out on the stage.)

(AEGLE follows them, but doesn't sit.)

ERYTHEIA. Aegle, we're going to have to check on the outer fields.

AEGLE. What?

ERYTHEIA. *(patiently)* The outer fields. The ones near Atlas. I think the irrigation system's down, because –

HESPERE. Yes, it is, I –

AEGLE. Erytheia, I am standing here, guarding the Golden Apples of Hera, the Queen of the Gods, and I am supposed to be thinking about *irrigation systems in the outer fields?*

ERYTHEIA. *(lightly)* Well, if you want to have food to eat, I suppose, but otherwise –

AEGLE. We live in the Garden of the Hesperides, beyond the sunset, and you think we're not going to have food? Mundanity has finally taken over your soul.

ERYTHEIA. *(still not losing her temper)* Fine, 'Spere and I will do it ourselves.

HESPERE. You have this argument every year.

AEGLE. I'm too busy guarding to argue.

ERYTHEIA. 'Spere, I *never* argue. And if mundanity has taken over my soul, it's only because I've got nothing better to *do* –

HESPERE. How about Aegle deflates her head a little bit, and Erytheia stops worrying so much. Then everything will be solved.

(Both glance at her fondly, clearly not taking her very seriously.)

Do you think you two would fight so much if we just had someone to go *("grown up voice")* Stop yelling!

(at the same time)

AEGLE. What, you mean like a –

ERYTHEIA. 'Spere –

HESPERE. I know. I'm not a baby. *(mimicking them)* "We haven't got parents."

*(**AEGLE** and **ERYTHEIA** sigh, as if this is a frequent topic of discussion.)*

(a pause)

HESPERE. Aegle, are you sure you're too busy guarding to argue?

AEGLE. Hespere, I'm concentrating.

HESPERE. Concentrating on what?

AEGLE. *(exasperated)* Guarding.

HESPERE. Oh. I thought you might be concentrating on something else.

AEGLE. Why?

HESPERE. Because you seem to have missed that man coming through the gates.

*(**AEGLE** looks angry.)*

*(**ERYTHEIA** raises her eyebrows, but doesn't look up from her book.)*

ERYTHEIA. 'Spere, the joke's gotten a little old, at this point.

AEGLE. Old? It's ancient, and it's not very funny. This is a serious job, which is something that neither of you seem to understand.

(She crosses her arms huffily, and then sneaks a look behind her.)

Oh Gods, there *is* a man at the gates.

*(**AEGLE** sprints offstage.)*

*(**ERYTHEIA** cranes her head to get a better look.)*

*(**HESPERE** doesn't seem particularly excited.)*

ERYTHEIA. There really is a man there. Well, I hope he walked through the outer fields, so he can tell Aegle that the irrigation system is broken.

(**AEGLE**, *walking very quickly, but trying to look dignified, enters.*)

AEGLE. (*grandly*) Sisters! I have news.

(**ERYTHEIA** *and* **HESPERE** *stare at her, nonplussed.*)

HESPERE. Why are you talking like that?

(**AEGLE** *jerks her head towards the place from which she's just come.* **ERYTHEIA** *and* **HESPERE**, *following her eyes, suddenly look shocked.*)

ERYTHEIA. (*whispering*) That isn't –

HESPERE. (*loud*) Is that the lion skin?

(**AEGLE** *and* **ERYTHEIA** *shush her.*)

AEGLE. Heracles, the son of Zeus, stands at our gate. He has reached our far off abode, despite great peril and travails. Now he begs that we admit him into our sacred garden, so he may ask a boon of us.

(**HESPERE** *is giggling.* **ERYTHEIA** *looks excited.*)

ERYTHEIA. (*hissing*) Let him in! Let him in!

AEGLE. Let us welcome him, and inform him of our duties, my fair comrades.

(**ERYTHEIA** *nods eagerly.* **HESPERE** *laughs louder.*)

(**AEGLE** *exits, and returns holding the hanger that is Heracles high above her head.*)

(**ERYTHEIA** *scrambles to her feet, pulling* **HESPERE** *after her. They stand behind* **AEGLE**, *facing the audience, in a pyramid formation.*)

(**AEGLE** *holds Heracles at an arm's length, looking very important.*)

AEGLE, ERYTHEIA, & HESPERE.
We live beyond the boundaries of Earth
Beyond the petty hopes and dreams of men
Whil'st you are here, we all will test your worth,
The undeserving, we send back again.

We may grant wishes to a worthy man,
But in one instance, he will find us hard,
We'll give him blessing that we can,
But not the apples Hera bade us guard.

*(**HESPERE** and **ERYTHEIA** step back and open the curtains to reveal the Tree, now glowing softly. Three Apples dangle from its branches, and Ladon is wrapped around its trunk. She gets back in formation. They continue, still in a ritual-esque style. As each says their line, they strike a pose.)*

HESPERE. When Hera married Zeus…

ERYTHEIA. The Earth, their grandmother, gave them a tree…

AEGLE. She planted it here, beyond the sunset, and told us we would be its guardians…

AEGLE, ERYTHEIA, & HESPERE. And so we have been to this day.

*(**ERYTHEIA** steps up so that she is level with **AEGLE**. She takes Heracles from **AEGLE**, who looks somewhat upstaged.)*

ERYTHEIA. I think we all know that you're worthy…what do you need?

Scene Three

*(**AEGLE** and **HESPERE** walk out – we are now in **ERYTHEIA**'s memory. She begins walking around the stage, showing Heracles the garden. Throughout the scene, she is very giddy.)*

ERYTHEIA. And these over here only bloom at twilight, so in a few minutes –

Are you looking at the Tree? I'm so used to it, that I hardly notice it anymore – but the Apples are beautiful. Thank you!

No, not much. I guess living all alone with your sisters, you don't get told very much that you're beautiful.

Oh, we've lived in the Garden for millennia. But I don't really see that we need to be guarding the tree at all. Ladon is enough – the serpent, wrapped around the tree.

Besides, the Apples are sort of useless by themselves. They give you immortality, but no one with mortal blood can pick them. And why would a god pick an Apple? They're already immortal.

I don't *mind* being here. And Aegle doesn't mind, it makes her feel important. But sometimes I think 'Spere minds a little. She talks a lot about our parents. Hera told us they were Nyx and Erebus, but we never met them.

No, I really don't mind. Well, not much. Just, you know, sometimes, I start to think, if maybe Hera'd chosen someone else...it's hard, all of us being together like this. We've all just become sort of – predictable. To ourselves, too. Sometimes I think I say things...just because Aegle or 'Spere think I'm going to say it.

*(**AEGLE** steps out and begins to sing. Her song is very beautiful.)*

Aegle's singing. We sing every sunset.

Oh, I'd much rather talk to you.

Well...all right. You really want to hear me?

*(**AEGLE** and **ERYTHEIA** sing together. When the song is over, **AEGLE** they both accompany Heracles offstage.)*

Scene Four

(The curtains are closed. **ERYTHEIA** *and* **HESPERE** *enter, holding hands.)*

HESPERE. The Sunset Song doesn't sound the same.

ERYTHEIA. Hm?

HESPERE. The Sunset Song. It sounds different, now that –

(She glances at the curtain, then at the ground.)

ERYTHEIA. Oh.

(They sit down.)

I just can't stop thinking, 'Spere – I talked with him for such a long time, and I'm worried that maybe I said things that I shouldn't have said, and that maybe one of the things I said was the reason that he was able to – to do this.

I just forgot. I forgot my job, I guess. And he was sitting there, and I'd heard so much about him, that I just – I just talked.

What if it's my fault?

HESPERE. *(softly)* It's not your fault.

It's my fault.

*(***ERYTHEIA*** looks surprised.)*

Scene Five

(The curtains are open, and the Tree has its Apples and Ladon. **HESPERE** *is sitting at its roots, smiling. She begins petting Ladon.* **AEGLE** *enters from stage.)*

AEGLE. Heracles! 'Spere, have you seen Heracles this morning? I can't find him.

*(***HESPERE** *shakes her head and then goes back to petting Ladon.)*

*(***ERYTHEIA** *enters.)*

Erytheia, have you seen Heracles?

*(***ERYTHEIA** *shakes her head, and yawns.)*

ERYTHEIA. Not since sunset. I showed him his room after the song.

AEGLE. He wouldn't just *leave*...he traveled to the ends of the Earth, he couldn't just leave...

ERYTHEIA. He kept on asking if he was any trouble. He's so polite. I'm sure that he's just trying to stay out of our way.

*(***ERYTHEIA** *smiles somewhat foolishly.)*

*(***AEGLE** *raises her eyebrows at her.)*

*(***ERYTHEIA** *looks guilty.)*

HESPERE. What? What's funny?

AEGLE & ERYTHEIA. Nothing.

HESPERE. Oh.

(She shrugs, and goes back to petting Ladon.)

*(***AEGLE** *and* **ERYTHEIA** *sit a little ways apart from her.)*

AEGLE. What did you talk about?

ERYTHEIA. Nothing really. Just what it's like here. That sort of thing. He's so modest, we barely talked about him at all.

AEGLE. Did you –

ERYTHEIA. *(quickly)* No!

AEGLE. I was going to say, "Ask if he really killed a lion with his bare hands." *(primly)* I know you were very curious about that.

ERYTHEIA. Oh. No. Um...no.

AEGLE. *(enviously)* It figures he would pick you.

ERYTHEIA. I don't know what you mean –

AEGLE. You're the prettiest, so of course he would pick you.

ERYTHEIA. Aegle!

(an awkward pause)

AEGLE. I'm just teasing. I didn't mean it.
Maybe he went to the outer fields. Do you want to go check?

ERYTHEIA. Okay...

(They get up and start to walk away, then turn back to **HESPERE.***)*

AEGLE. 'Spere, will you be all right watching the tree for a while?

*(***HESPERE*** nods.)*

*(***AEGLE*** and ***ERYTHEIA*** exit stage left, arm in arm.)*

HESPERE. *(speaking to Ladon)* They get stupid around boys.
I think he's pretty stupid, with that lion skin. It's just showing off.

"Hi, I'm Heracles. Look at me! I have so many muscles, that there's no room for my brain to function."

"Oh, Heracles! Who needs a brain anyway!"

"Well, I've come to the ends of the Earth, and I won't tell you why, but let me come in and eat all your food and guzzle down some thousand year old wine."

"Oh, sure, Heracles! It's not like we have anything better to do anyway! No, the gods won't be eternally wrathful if we screw up, because they're just nice like that!"

*(***HESPERE*** cracks herself up.)*

HESPERE. *(cont.)* I think snakes are better than people, anyway. They should just go and follow Heracles around, or something. I'd be fine here.

*(**HESPERE** jerks quickly to look offstage.)*

Who's there?

Oh…Heracles…

(She exits, and comes back on immediately holding the hanger that is Heracles.)

Um…good morning…Erytheia isn't here right now, but she's looking for you in the outer –

(A pause as she tries figure out a way to get rid of him.)

Well, are you *sure* you wouldn't rather tell Erytheia? What?

(A pause. Whatever he's said has shocked her.)

No! That's just not – that's not – *how could he be my father?*

But if you freed him for us, wouldn't the Gods get mad?

Well then – then I want to help.

Oh, no. No, I couldn't do that. I can't – what if Aegle found out, or what if –

You'll really bring him to us? You promise?

*(A moment as she makes a decision. With resolve, she goes back to the Tree and picks the Apples. **HESPERE** exits with Heracles. This is when we hear the Sunset Song. When the Sunset Song finishes, the Tree stops glowing.)*

Scene Seven

(The curtains are open. The tree is bare. **HESPERE** *is hunched at its roots, holding the dead Ladon close to her face.)*

HESPERE. *(cont.)* Ladon. *Ladon.*

*(***ERYTHEIA*** enters. She helps* **HESPERE** *get up. They embrace.)*

*(***AEGLE*** enters.)*

HESPERE. He said that he needed the Apples, and then he'd be able to free him. Our father. He said our father was a prisoner, and he needed them so that the gods wouldn't be wrathful, and I just couldn't tell you, not when you were screaming and fighting…and Ladon…

ERYTHEIA. But 'Spere, why did you tell us that you were looking for Ladon?

HESPERE. I was. I was looking for his body.

AEGLE. Why would he do this?

ERYTHEIA. *(Her voice is flat.)* That's what heroes do. They steal…

(A pause as she thinks about what to say.)

Things.

HESPERE. The plants are dying. Just like Ladon died.

ERYTHEIA. I know. I think the Apples kept them all alive.

HESPERE. Then will we also –

ERYTHEIA. I don't think so. Although when Hera finds out about this…

AEGLE. I'm sorry. This is all my fault. I'm the oldest, I'm supposed to –

HESPERE. Will you stop that? Just because you're the oldest, you're not the one who's supposed to take care of everything, and because I'm the youngest, that doesn't mean I'm the baby. We didn't trust each other, and now it's too late.

But how did he *know*…how did he know that I wanted our father to come back…

ERYTHEIA. When I was – talking – with him, I think I said, I think I said that you thought about our parents... Hespere...

AEGLE. I shouldn't have let him in in the first place. But I thought that was my job. Our job.

ERYTHEIA. We failed. That's it. We just failed. Do you think we'll get punished?

AEGLE. If the Apples aren't here, and the garden is dying, then...what do we do? We're not guardians anymore.

(They all pause. Then **HESPERE** *gets up.)*

HESPERE. We leave.

Let's go, I mean it. Let's just go. What's keeping us here anymore?

*(***AEGLE*** and* **ERYTHEIA** *rise hesitantly.)*

ERYTHEIA. Leave...the garden. That's a thought.

I wish – we had never been guardians. It wasn't fair, it was never fair –

HESPERE. Since when are the Gods fair?

AEGLE. We'll...we'll stay together, won't we?

Oh. Well. Good then.

So...we just won't live beyond the sunset.

(All three hold hands. They take a few steps, then turn back to look at the dead Tree.)

(A pause.)

(Blackout.)

KEEPING COMPANY

by Michael Bontatibus

PRODUCTION HISTORY

KEEPING COMPANY was first produced by Youth Theatre Northwest in April 2009 and was directed by Michael Bontatibus. The cast was as follows:

RICHARD .... Nathan Lessler
DAN/CUDDLES .... Spencer Hamp
EILEEN/ELFIE .... Clara Flaherty
NORMAN/LUCKY .... Thomas Rodgers

CHARACTER BREAKDOWN

RICHARD – CEO, in theory. Nervous, submissive, low self-esteem. Age range 30+. (M)

DAN – Ringleader, alpha male. Enjoys agitating Richard. Age range 20-40. (M)

EILEEN – Queen bitch. Very passive-aggressive. Age range 20-40. (F)

NORMAN – Follower, although he is significantly older than the rest. Grins all the time. Age range 30-50. (M)

CUDDLES – Parallel to Dan. Intelligent, manipulative, always assuring. (M)

ELFIE – Parallel to Eileen. (F)

LUCKY – Parallel to Norman. (M)

ABOUT THE PLAYWRIGHT

Keeping Company is Michael Bontatibus's first play, written when he was a sophomore at Mercer Island High School in Washington State. It was produced and directed by him as part of the Fringe program at Youth Theatre Northwest in 2009, where he has been acting since he was young. His second play, Laugh Track, was part of the subsequent year's program. He is currently writing his first full-length play, which further exhibits his affinity for dark humor.

Scene One

*(RICHARD enters unimpressive: hunched over, trying to carry several folders, a newspaper, a briefcase, and a latte in his hands at the same time. His hair is neatly combed, he wears a shirt with the collar and tie nearly choking him, his pants are a little too short. Everything about him screams uptight. He comes to the door to his office building, attempting to fish his keys out of his pocket without spilling any of his accessories, finally managing to get them and unlock the door. Lights up on the stage: his coworkers, **DAN**, **EILEEN**, and **NORMAN**. **DAN** reeks of sleaziness, **EILEEN** is dressed to kill, and **NORMAN** holds an obnoxious grin on his face redolent of the Cheshire Cat. They sit around a table, talking as though they have just finished a long conversation and are now simply killing time. **RICHARD** is startled to see the three there.)*

RICHARD. Oh. Hey, guys.

*(**NORMAN** grunts. Beat.)*

Am I late?

*(Upon receiving no answer, **RICHARD** looks at his watch.)*

No…I thought the meeting wasn't for another hour.

NORMAN. Ah, well…

DAN. *(faking friendliness to the point where he's subtly mocking **RICHARD**)* We were all here, so we figured, why not get started?

*(Pause. **RICHARD** stands there dumbly.)*

RICHARD. So, you reached a decision then?

NORMAN. Yep, we decided to close the deal.

EILEEN. *(extremely passive-aggressive)* We went ahead because we all knew you were leaning that direction anyway.

(**RICHARD** *opens and closes his mouth – he was not leaning in that direction.*)

DAN. Just need you to sign this.

(**DAN** *slides a sheet of paper and a pen* **RICHARD***'s way.*)

RICHARD. Ah. Umm…okay. Okay. *(He signs the papers.)*

DAN. Thanks, Rich.

(Lights change to indicate elapsed time. **RICHARD** *sits at his desk. Listening to the others talk, he decides to be bold for a day and bring a chair over and join the discussion.)*

NORMAN. Maybe we just shouldn't reply. Let them consult a few other companies, make them realize we're they're best option.

EILEEN. That works if we *are* their best option.

NORMAN. It's taking a gamble, yeah, but if they do choose us it'll pay off big time. If they don't, we have other customers.

DAN. I'm sick of Prentice and Co. Honestly, I say we go with Norm's plan, and if they don't take the deal, screw 'em.

RICHARD. Wait, guys, these have been good customers of ours for a while, and –

EILEEN. *(not missing a beat)* I like it, I like it. So, we'll just do…nothing.

DAN. Richard, that's okay with you, right?

(All look at **RICHARD***. Their gazes bore into him, indicating that they all know what his answer has to be.* **RICHARD** *nods compliantly. Lights shift again, indicating another time change.* **NORMAN** *and* **DAN** *are gone.* **EILEEN** *walks in to* **RICHARD** *at his desk, unpacking his things.)*

EILEEN. Rich, you need to sign these.

RICHARD. Okay, I'll look at them today.

*(**DAN** walks in and leans against the doorway, smugly supervising.)*

EILEEN. Rich… *(come on, buddy, you know the drill)* I need you to sign these. *(beat)*

RICHARD. Okay.

*(He does so. **DAN** walks further into the room and sits down. He looks around like he's forgotten something, going so far as to pat his torso, overacting in preparation for his next act of malice.)*

DAN. Ooh. Damn. Oh, hey, Rich?

RICHARD. Yeah?

DAN. Do you think you could grab me a cup of coffee?

*(**RICHARD** stares ahead, almost stunned. **DAN** has gone to demoting him to an intern, something he hasn't quite done before. But to **RICHARD**, there's really only one answer.)*

RICHARD. Sure.

DAN. Thanks a lot, Rich.

Scene Two

*(**RICHARD** walks into his apartment, which is roughly as impressive as he is. A dirty plate and glass still lie on a table, which is the only piece of furniture in the room other than a couple chairs. Front lights should be dimmed, so that shadows within reasonable limits are cast on **RICHARD**'s face. Other lights are blue, white, making this a dark, ominous place, a place where no good things happen. **RICHARD** dumps his briefcase at the foot of his chair and collapses in it, burying his face in his hands. This has been one of the worse days. He gets up, pacing, frustrated at himself, at his helplessness in his situation. Through all of this, **CUDDLES**, **ELFIE**, and **LUCKY**, three classically cute stuffed animals, rise up unnoticed. Their voices are seductive in a childlike way, high-pitched and harmonic, like chimes, but still reminiscent of each of their co-worker parallels: **DAN**, **EILEEN**, and **NORMAN**, respectively.)*

CUDDLES. You know, Richard, I can help.

*(Long pause. **RICHARD** is distraught. Things have gone from what he thought was bad to the worst possible. He fumbles for words for a moment.)*

RICHARD. I thought…I thought you left.

CUDDLES. We never go away.

RICHARD. The doctor said –

ELFIE. We know. We were listening. On the phone.

RICHARD. *(softly)* Oh.

ELFIE. Don't listen to your doctors, Rich. They're not good people.

RICHARD. Yes –

LUCKY. No, they're not. I mean, they tried to kill us.

*(**RICHARD** is silent. Beat.)*

They did.

RICHARD. That's…that's not what they were trying to do.

LUCKY. *(sighing)* Yeah, we know.

ELFIE. But we're here now. What's going on? It's been so long.

(**RICHARD** *struggles with the idea of changing the subject, but does so.*)

RICHARD. Well...the business...the business got big, bigger than I could have ever hoped for. And I got three new people on board. (*unenthusiastically, forced*) They're a big help.

CUDDLES. You don't sound too excited about them.

RICHARD. It was a...bad call, on my part.

LUCKY. Why is that?

RICHARD. They're...they're sort of mea– well, they're not *mean*, they just don't really understand how I'm –

CUDDLES. They *understand* fine, Richard. They just don't care.

ELFIE. You can be straightforward with us, Richard. We're not going anywhere. Your secrets stay with us.

LUCKY. Always. (*pause*)

RICHARD. I...it's been difficult. When we started expanding, I brought on Eileen, and I thought she could help, and she did to the point where I had to bring on Norman, and then I found that I wasn't really...I didn't have a lot of influence, so I brought on Dan to help me out. And from there... (*beat*)

ELFIE. Are you afraid of them?

RICHARD. No, no, that's not the right word. Just...intimidated a little, they don't respect me, they don't listen to my ideas, which aren't that great, but still, they – they sit in my office all day because it's...bigger. It's just a little rude.

ELFIE. We're sorry to hear that.

RICHARD. It's just been hard, I don't get a lot of say anymore.

LUCKY. Are you not making money anymore?

RICHARD. Money's fine. But I enjoy running the business, I *did* enjoy running the business. It's always been my passion, you know that.

CUDDLES. Yes, yes we do. We understand you. *(pause)*

RICHARD. No, you don't.

CUDDLES. We do.

RICHARD. *(almost laughing)* No, no you don't, because you're stuffed animals! *(somewhat angrily)* This is ridiculous, I thought I was done with you!

CUDDLES. We never go away.

RICHARD. Apparently.

ELFIE. Don't beat yourself up, Richard.

(**LUCKY** *attempts to steer the conversation away from their unlikely existence.*)

LUCKY. You don't need to talk about us. We've been here.

ELFIE. Not much to tell.

LUCKY. Tell us more about you.

CUDDLES. Your business partners, can you fire them?

RICHARD. I can, yeah. But I don't want to, even though they're...not really nice to me all the time, they're good at what they do. They've gotten the business farther than I could have ever gotten it on my own. If I got rid of any one of them, I wouldn't know how to handle it.

ELFIE. I think you could.

RICHARD. How would you know? You're, you're a stuff –

CUDDLES. How about we revisit this later?

LUCKY. *(hurriedly)* Sounds good to me.

ELFIE. Richard, we don't want you getting pushed around. We're your friends.

(**RICHARD** *laughs bitterly. There is a long pause.*)

CUDDLES. *(kindly)* Why don't you sit down. Tell us everything.

(**RICHARD** *sighs and sits in the chair.*)

Scene Three

(**RICHARD** *walks into his office.* **NORMAN, DAN,** *and* **EILEEN** *sit around their usual table, talking.*)

RICHARD. Hey, everyone.

(*The three continue talking.* **RICHARD** *stops where he is and forcibly looks straight ahead, not at any of his co-workers.* **RICHARD** *clears his throat, speaks louder.*)

Hey, everyone.

ALL EXCEPT RICHARD. Hi, Rich. Richard. Hey, Richard.

(**RICHARD** *tries to hide a smile. He breaks into a confident stride and sits down at his desk very happily. He pulls out his laptop and begins typing, chuckling to himself. Others give him looks, but do no more.* **RICHARD** *gets up, grabs a coffee mug, and almost skips offstage.*)

Scene Four

*(**RICHARD**'s house. He is elated, pacing with a big grin on his face.)*

RICHARD. I really think that's the first time anyone has said hi to me in the morning!

CUDDLES. Good. Did you do any of that other stuff that we told you to do?

RICHARD. Ah, no, no. I didn't want to push it. But it's almost invigorating, I actually got a response.

LUCKY. *(slightly dissatisfied)* So…they said hi, and that's it.

RICHARD. *(not understanding why* **LUCKY** *is disappointed)* Yeah…

CUDDLES. It's a good…start, yes, but you'll need to do a little better than that.

ELFIE. You need to gain their respect.

RICHARD. I know, yeah, but I have to take it slow.

CUDDLES. *(comforting again)* Okay…but here's what I think you should do tomorrow. I think you should go in there, and actively join their conversation. I don't care whether it's about business or anyone's personal life, just join the conversation. And *make* yourself a part of it. *Make* them acknowledge you.

RICHARD. No, no, they really won't like that.

LUCKY. Then they'll have to deal with it. You're the boss.

RICHARD. *(attempting to crack a bitter joke)* Not anymore.

ELFIE. Well with that kind of attitude, you'll never be in control again! *(struggling to remember)* Look, they're the…the vice president of…

RICHARD. VP of Sales, VP of Operations, VP of Finance.

CUDDLES. Right. And you're the CEO.

LUCKY. It's not their job to run the company, but they're doing it anyway.

CUDDLES. They've been awful to you, and yet you're worried about upsetting them by joining their *conversation*?

*(**RICHARD** nods, smiles a little bit.)*

RICHARD. Okay.

Scene Five

*(**RICHARD** walks into his office. He looks at the three sitting around the table and takes a deep breath. He sets his briefcase down, grabs a chair, and sits down at the table with the rest of them. They give him a look, and proceed in their conversation, ignoring him.)*

DAN. Fact of the matter is, Rob's been lazy. He's been behind on his work, he's been calling in "sick" *very* frequently for the past couple months –

RICHARD. Well what if he –

DAN. And frankly, I don't like his attitude. We've given him warning enough, and a business can't survive with bad employees!

RICHARD. *(under his breath)* Evidently, it can.

EILEEN. What?

RICHARD. Ah, nothing.

EILEEN. *("That's what I thought.")* Uh-huh.

RICHARD. Well, hang on guys, I know Rob, I hired him personally, I can talk to him if you guys want.

NORMAN. Um.

*(Beat. There's a dilemma, it would take a problem off their hands, but they'd be granting **RICHARD** power, something they haven't done in a long time. And yet...)*

DAN. Okay. Okay, fine, if you want to deal with this slacker, then be my guest.

EILEEN. Oh, Rich, I need you to sign these.

RICHARD. Okay. Um, let me just read them really fast.

*(**EILEEN** gives a drawn-out, exasperated sigh. **RICHARD** skims them as fast as he can.)*

RICHARD. Okay, they look good. *(He signs the papers.)*

Scene Six

*(**RICHARD** has just finished telling a story, very pleased with himself.)*

ELFIE. Good job!

RICHARD. And – I sort of read something they gave me before I signed it.

LUCKY. Okay, that's good too.

RICHARD. Wow. Thanks, guys, really. That was a good idea, that was, that was genius.

ELFIE. Aww, you're welcome.

CUDDLES. *(treading ever so delicately)* Next, however, you've got to step it up a bit. What I want you to do might get them a little angry.

RICHARD. *(apprehensive)* Okay...

CUDDLES. Go in there, and directly contradict, or do the opposite of whatever they want to do. I don't care if it's a good idea.

RICHARD. They have to be reminded that you're the ultimate authority! That, in the end, everything gets approved because you choose to approve it.

*(**RICHARD** slowly nods, then upgrades it to a quick nod, furrowing his brow in agreement.)*

RICHARD. Yeah. Yeah. You're right.

LUCKY. Go get 'em.

Scene Seven

(RICHARD strides into work, the other trio at their usual table.)

RICHARD. Hi, everyone.

(The others mumble greetings. RICHARD sits down at his desk, EILEEN gets up and walks up to him.)

EILEEN. Richard, you need to sign this.

(Beat as an ultimatum approaches. RICHARD steels himself and takes a deep breath.)

RICHARD. No!

(Pause. NORMAN and DAN turn around to look at what's happening.)

EILEEN. Richard, this is Gladys's retirement card. *(pause)*

RICHARD. *(high-pitched)* Oh.

(RICHARD is mortified. If he doesn't do something uncharacteristically confident fast, he'd be set back so far in his progress he wouldn't know how to start again. RICHARD knows this, and struggles with it. He signs the card, then throws the pen back down on the table unnecessarily hard.)

RICHARD. There you go.

EILEEN. And, you need to approve these.

(EILEEN slides a stack of papers onto his desk.)

RICHARD. What's this, the deal with Glencoe?

EILEEN. Yep.

RICHARD. I don't want to. *(RICHARD is trembling.)*

EILEEN. Excuse me?

RICHARD. I don't want to approve it. I don't like the way this is going. I've heard terrible things from other companies about dealing with these guys.

*(Although **RICHARD** planned to go against anything they did, he does have the upper hand of honesty here: he*

has heard bad things about this company. **EILEEN** *looks to* **NORMAN** *and* **DAN** *for help. They both approach the desk.)*

EILEEN. Richard, you agreed to this already.

RICHARD. I changed my mind!

NORMAN. We've already put money into making this go through!

DAN. You cannot, you *cannot* back out now!

RICHARD. Yes, I can!

NORMAN. Okay, well, you *can*, but…

*(***DAN** *and* **EILEEN** *glare at* **NORMAN**. **NORMAN** *is, indeed, the weakest link here – if* **RICHARD** *was gone,* **NORMAN** *would be the one they'd turn on.* **NORMAN** *quickly attempts to salvage his sentence.)*

B-but it'd be a terrible idea! We've been negotiating with Glencoe for the past week and a half!

DAN. Do you want our company to be known for breaking deals?!

EILEEN. Just sign the paper!

NORMAN. You can't break the deal now of all times!

*(***RICHARD** *is visibly overwhelmed. He gets up as the others are shouting at him and walks towards the door, trying to talk over their shouts.)*

RICHARD. I've made…I've made my decision. I think I should go, I have business, I can't, I have to leave.

*(***RICHARD** *exits. The shouting stops.* **DAN** *punches the desk.)*

DAN. Damn it!

Scene Eight

(**RICHARD** *walks in briskly.*)

RICHARD. *(quickly)* I don't know if that was a good idea.

LUCKY. What, what happened?

RICHARD. They yelled at me.

ELFIE. Aww.

CUDDLES. Hey, Rich. Rich! Come on, what are they doing, yelling at you? You're their boss! They have absolutely no right to do that! *They* should be intimidated by *you*!

RICHARD. Yeah, I know.

CUDDLES. Now, I want you to go back there and assert yourself!

LUCKY. Show them who's boss.

RICHARD. I don't really want to go back there today.

CUDDLES. Rich. Go back there. Now. *(pause)*

RICHARD. Okay.

(*Lights down as* **RICHARD** *composes himself.*)

Scene 9

(RICHARD *walks into his office.* EILEEN, DAN, *and* NORM *are sitting, idly chatting, albeit with a more serious atmosphere. Upon seeing him, all rise and start talking simultaneously.*)

ALL EXCEPT RICHARD. *(ad lib.)* What the hell are you thinking? I had the Glencoe CEO on the phone a second ago, he wants to talk to you. In all my years of business, this has got to be the worst move I've ever seen.

RICHARD. Okay, okay, OKAY!

(*All fall quiet.* RICHARD *is leaning on his desk, very flustered.*)

You know, this won't kill us.

DAN. It might as well. This is a huge deal, a *huge* deal.

RICHARD. *(looking down at the floor, stuttering)* I'm in charge, and I think we should not go through with this.

DAN. *(aggressively)* Why?

(RICHARD *doesn't have a good reason on hand, and* DAN *knows it.*)

RICHARD. B-because, I think they're not really –

(DAN *nods sarcastically.*)

DAN. Yeah, yeah, screw this. I'm calling Glencoe, I'm closing this deal.

RICHARD. No, you're not. I'm the CEO here.

DAN. *(sarcastic)* Oh yeah, and you're just doing beautifully. I'll be in my office.

RICHARD. Dan, get back here.

DAN. *(tauntingly as he walks away)* It'll just be a minute.

RICHARD. Dan! You are way out of line!

(RICHARD *tries to get his attention while* DAN *yells at him. Although* DAN *hasn't been suppressing his true feelings about* RICHARD *like* RICHARD *has about the other co-workers,* DAN *still bursts like a dam – now is the opportune time to just say straight out how much of an idiot failure he thinks* **RICHARD** *is.)*

RICHARD. Dan...Dan...Dan...

DAN. Me?! I'm out of line! I don't know what's going through your head right now, I'm doing what's best for the company! I don't know why you have a problem now of all times, but I'm not listening to you when you clearly don't know what you're doing!

RICHARD. Dan, you're FIRED!

(long silence)

DAN. What? Screw that. I'm...I'm calling Glencoe.

RICHARD. I'm not kidding. Get out.

*(***DAN*** laughs.)*

DAN. No.

RICHARD. Norman, call security.

*(***DAN*** looks pointedly at* **NORMAN.** **NORMAN** *avoids both men's gaze and looks at the floor in front of him.)*

NORMAN. That...that's not my job, I –

RICHARD. Call security.

*(***NORMAN*** looks at* **RICHARD,** *and then* **DAN,** *and then* **RICHARD** *again.)*

NORMAN. Okay.

*(***EILEEN*** looks scared. She leaves after* **NORMAN** *does, both decidedly not looking at* **DAN.** **DAN** *glares at* **RICHARD** *for a long, silent moment.* **RICHARD** *returns eye contact defiantly, the entire time.* **DAN** *realizes he's lost, but leaves trying to retain what dignity he has left.* **RICHARD** *exhales loudly.)*

Scene 10

(Lights slowly fade up. **RICHARD** *is sitting without his blazer, tie loosened, collar unbuttoned. A long period of time has passed.)*

RICHARD. Guys...I can't thank you enough, really.

ELFIE. Aww, you're welcome.

RICHARD. I just want to say... *(pause)*

LUCKY. Yes?

*(***RICHARD*** laughs.)*

RICHARD. Sorry. It's been so long since I've...addressed... this. I just want to say...I'm sorry I got those doctors to try and get rid of you. I mean, you never told me to steal anything or kill anybody. You never asked me to do anything bad, you only helped me out, no layers or alternative motives. Completely selflessly. You just tried to help.

CUDDLES. It's okay, Rich. Don't worry about it at all. And now everything's right again. We're all friends again, and now you're *completely* in control.

RICHARD. Yeah.

CUDDLES. Now...Do you think you could grab me a cup of tea?

*(***RICHARD*** pauses. This is strangely familiar to him, like a sense of déjà vu. This command has a negative connotation, and* **RICHARD**, *on some level knows this. And yet to* **RICHARD**, *there's really only one answer.)*

RICHARD. Sure.

(blackout)

SO

by Zoë Wilson

CHARACTER BREAKDOWN

ETHAN
TEGAN
NURSE
JUDI
DOCTOR

ABOUT THE PLAYWRIGHT

Zoë Wilson wrote *So* with one thought in mind: how one person's life can be viewed so drastically different by the ones in it. She hopes that it's something everyone thinks about when they experience *So*. *So* is Zoë's first play, but you can rest assured that you'll be hearing more from her soon.

Scene One

(Open on a busy E.R. room. **ETHAN** *is already sitting centerstage with his head in his hands. Like everyone else in the room his head snaps up anytime someone enters the stage right door, hoping that it's a* **DOCTOR** *with news. It never seems to be.)*

(Finally stage left door flings open and **TEGAN** *bursts into the room. She's in pajama pants, her hair in a wild pony tail. It's clear that she has been launched from bed. She looks around frantically and finally her eyes land on* **ETHAN** *as he stands. She runs to him and is about to strike his chest, but he catches her into a bear hug. Holding her tightly and burying his face in her hair.* **TEGAN** *struggles against* **ETHAN** *the whole time.)*

ETHAN. Tea, calm down. Tegan, come on! Stop it. Calm down, please.

TEGAN. Let me go!

*(***TEGAN** *finally struggles her way out of* **ETHAN***s grasp. Pushing him away from her, clearly angry. For a moment they stare each other down.* **TEGAN** *glaring at* **ETHAN**, **ETHAN** *carefully watching her. Finally,* **TEGAN** *slumps down into a chair and lets out a slight sob.)*

TEGAN. How could you, Ethan? How could you?!

ETHAN. It was just a party, Tea. I didn't know that this was gonna happen.

*(***ETHAN** *sits as well, and tries to put an arm around* **TEGAN** *but she flinches away. Her face disgusted.)*

TEGAN. You didn't know? I think you could of guessed Ethan!

ETHAN. It's just that he's been sober for so long and–

TEGAN. EXACTLY, Ethan! He'd been sober for so long. So obviously if he was thrown into an environment with alcohol everywhere then he's going to drink it! Have you really lost that many brain cells that you couldn't think of that?

ETHAN. Of course I thought it...But–

TEGAN. But what, Ethan?! But what?

ETHAN. He begged me to take him somewhere. He just wanted to have some fun. We agreed two beers tops but then he got out of my sight and...

TEGAN. Oh my god.

(TEGAN *turns away from him disgusted, then her eyes land on the person that just entered stage left. It's* JUDI, *Kaden's mother. Shooting up,* TEGAN *rushes towards* JUDI *and throws herself into her arms. The two hug tightly.*)

(ETHAN *watches them for a moment, wanting to be part of the moment but knowing full well that he's not welcome. He turns his head stage right where the* NURSE *enters he crosses to her quickly pushing through the crowd that surrounds her.*)

ETHAN. Please. Kaden Rockwell. Anything?

NURSE. Please sit down, sir. We'll call you when we have news.

(ETHAN *sighs and turns away as the* NURSE *turns to other patients. He looks up and makes brief eye contact with* JUDI *before quickly looking away and slowly shuffling towards the duo. It's clear that it's two against one.*)

ETHAN. I'm so sorry, Judi. I –

(JUDI *turns away from him without a word. Taking* TEGAN*'s hand in her own and moving away from the boy.* TEGAN *barely looks at him. Defeated,* ETHAN *goes and slumps down in a seat in the corner as the* NURSE *exits.*)

TEGAN. Where's Denny?

JUDI. Colorado on business, but he's trying to catch the red eye right now to get here…Is there any news?

TEGAN. Not that I know of. Only what Ethan told us on the phone.

JUDI. Well, what did he tell you?

*(**TEGAN** sighs and wrings her hands together.)*

TEGAN. I can't imagine it would be much different from what he told you.

JUDI. Tegan.

*(**TEGAN** hesitates a moment longer before speaking.)*

TEGAN. He just said that they had gone to a party, and that Kaden drank way too much, and he left without telling anyone. He said once he realized Kaden was gone, he left the party too. But Kaden had taken the car…

*(**TEGAN** gets choked up.)*

He had to wait till someone could drive him, and they found Kaden in Ethan's car in a ditch off fifth Avenue.

*(It's clear this is too much for **TEGAN**, and she buries her face in her hands and starts to sob. **JUDI** nods slowly and rubs **TEGAN**'s back.)*

JUDI. Yes. That's what he told me, too.

*(After a moment **JUDI** stands and starts to cross to **ETHAN**. He looks up at her and she stops. Turning away, **JUDI** crosses back to **TEGAN**, sitting next to her and rubbing her back. She starts to speak, but **TEGAN** doesn't react. **JUDI** delivers an inner monologue that no one can hear but the audience.)*

Scene Two

JUDI. So...In a way it's funny because I always thought that this type of thing only happened to people that lead dramatic lives. You know the story...like when...the couple that can never have kids finally has their miracle baby. Then they get divorced down the line. Then because of the divorce, their kid becomes an alcoholic and gets in a car accident because his stupid friend took him to a party while he was recovering. This type of thing isn't suppose to happen in real life. In a well-planned life. We planned Kaden. We adored him. We close to spoiled him!

(She starts to twist her wedding ring and stands.)

Kaden had such a good childhood. Denny and I knew we only wanted one child and we stuck to that. We lived in a good neighborhood. With good people and good schools. All through elementary school Kaden got good grades. He liked school more than most kids, but he wasn't the greatest at it. *(She smiles softly.)* He wasn't by any means a quiet child either. He loved talking and asking questions. He had a lot of friends, not many really close ones, but not many kids do at that age. I mean. He had a normal healthy childhood. It's still hard to try and remember where it went wrong. When things got bad. Elementary school flew by with no problem and junior high rolled around. Kaden did become less involved in school. Not as interested in the work. Which wasn't that bad of a thing. His grades went from high A's to B's and high C's. I didn't think much of it. I guess that's where things turned though. He bonded with a group by the end of seventh grade... All boys have to have a group so I didn't worry. I didn't even worry once he gained his best friend. Ethan. *(She laughs bitterly.)* I guess I should of worried. But I was happy for my boy. Happy that he had found his people. I thought it'd be good for him. In fact I was sure of it. But...slowly my outgoing little boy became a withdrawn teenager. I didn't know what to do about it but I went with it. Teenagers were always withdrawn right? It didn't mean anything. The worry didn't set in till his sophomore year when his grades started to drop and he started coming home late. But my worry was too late in coming by then. My baby boy was already far gone.

Scene Three

*(The **NURSE** enters stage right again, and this time **TEGAN** rushes to the woman. Before **TEGAN** has a chance to talk the **NURSE** puts up a hand to stop her. **JUDI** crosses back to her seat.)*

NURSE. Ma'am, please sit. If I call the name of your patient then I have news for you, otherwise, I can't help you. I'm sorry we're very busy.

*(The **NURSE** turns away from **TEGAN**.)*

Miller? Britney Miller?

*(Another family jumps up and rushes to hear their news, **TEGAN** slumps and crosses back to **JUDI** as defeated as ever.)*

JUDI. What did she say?

TEGAN. Nothing. They're very busy. If she calls our patients name then she'll have news for us.

*(As **TEGAN** talks, she dissolves into tears. Turning to bury her face in **JUDI**'s shoulder.)*

JUDI. Shhh ,shhh. It'll be okay.

*(The other woman takes the girl into a motherly embrace, nervously twisting her wedding ring behind **TEGAN**'s back. It should be becoming clear that the only reason **JUDI** isn't crying is because she's trying to be strong for **TEGAN**. Meanwhile **ETHAN** watches this scene helplessly. He stands and slowly crosses to the women.)*

ETHAN. Do you guys need anything…water or something?

*(**JUDI** surveys the boy then slowly nods.)*

JUDI. Waters would be nice. If you're sure you can handle that *(her voice becomes bitter)* without getting drunk.

*(**ETHAN** flinches but says nothing. He exits stage right.)*

Scene Four

*(**ETHAN** re-enters through the center of the curtain and move downstage right. He talks to the audience, but pantomimes as though he's getting items from the vending machine.)*

ETHAN. So I just love how those two also have to blame everything on me. Every problem in Kaden's life is my fault!

(He reaches in his pocket for his wallet to get change out. As he talks he slowly switches between feeding the change into the slot, pressing in numbers, and bending to grab the items dropped.)

Nothing bad in Kad's life could every have just been his choice. Oh no. All me. Sure I went with him to that party, but…god, and Judi! Ugh, that woman just thinks her son is so perfect. Like all his good grades always came easy to him. Like he actually liked school. Like his life only started going downhill because of all the peer pressure from me. *(He rolls his eyes.)* She could just never take the time to realize how hard he worked his whole childhood to make her happy. He always loved his parents so much. He just liked seeing them smile. I still remember the day we met in junior high. Kaden was in the bathroom practically hyperventilating because he had just found out he had gotten a C for the semester and he was so sure his parents would kill him. Or worse, not smile! I told him to calm down, that it'd be fine. Then the next day he comes prancing up to me with this story about how his mom had pat him on the back and said that he did great, that junior high was harder than elementary school. So I guess the fact that my good advice had been right was the thing that sealed our friendship. *(He laughs.)* I actually had really liked Judi back then, she was a nice woman that deserved her son's love. Then high school started. It's funny because Judi thinks the drinking was my fault… but Kaden was the one that egged me into going to our first party. Kaden was the one that put a red cup of beer into my hand. That's how it started. At first we just got drunk at parties on Saturdays like other teenagers. But slowly Kaden started to drink more and more. He'd be drunk on Fridays, to "pre-game himself" as he would say. Then on Sundays, to "chase the hangovers away." Then he started drinking during the week to get through classes. I didn't know why he drank so much, and I was just a stupid kid so I didn't try to stop him. I didn't understand addiction. Heck, sometimes I'd join him. We drank away our four years of high school together. But when college rolled around and I started to get it together, Kaden just...couldn't. That's when he went to recovery. Finally. I guess there was just something in him that likes the liquor...some monster. Something that needs on it. Feeds on it. I could almost see it...this raging monster in his eyes when he asked to go to this party as my wedding gift to him.

(He starts toward the exit, pantomiming carrying bottles. He stops right at the curtain and half turns.)

Do you know how hard it is to say no to an addict when they beg you? *(He chuckles bitterly.)* I guess I just can't say no to my best friend.

(He exits through the curtain.)

Scene Five

(**ETHAN** *re-enters stage right. He is now carrying three real water bottles and a few chip bags. It's clear on everyones faces that they are disappointed that he's not the* **NURSE**. **TEGAN** *is still buried in* **JUDI***'s shoulder as* **ETHAN** *crosses to them.*)

ETHAN. Here. I got some food, too.

JUDI. 'Kay. Put it down.

(**JUDI** *nods to the chair next to her, and* **ETHAN** *obeys with everything except one bottle. He cracks it open and takes a swig of water as he watches* **JUDI** *rubbing* **TEGAN***'s heaving back. Slowly, he moves to sit on the other side of* **TEGAN**. *At the same time the* **NURSE** *and the* **DOCTOR** *enter stage right.* **TEGAN**, *as well as everyone else, looks to them.*)

NURSE. Wells? Adam Wells?

(*The trio sighs, half in relief, half in disappointment, and looks away as the 'Wells' family rushes to hear the news.*)

ETHAN. Listen, Tea...

(*He goes to put a hand on her back but she jumps up and turns on him. Screaming madly:*)

TEGAN. NO! You listen Ethan. This is all your fault! What kind of person takes a alcoholic to a party two weeks before the biggest day of their lives? Do you not think? Our wedding is coming up Ethan! OUR WEDDING!! If he dies –

(*She chokes on the word, breaking into a sob, she runs out the door stage right. Seeing* **ETHAN***'s distraught face* **JUDI** *reaches across the empty chair to him.*)

JUDI. She's just in shock.

(*The curtain closes as* **ETHAN** *takes* **JUDI***'s hand, tears welling in both of their eyes.*)

Scene Six

*(**TEGAN** runs onstage and crosses into the bathroom. She should pantomime standing at the sink and splashing her face with water, like the vending machine this is towards the audience. Looking up into the mirror she bites her lip.)*

TEGAN. So...if he dies my life is ruined. *(Her head slumps down for a moment before she looks back up with a slight smile.)* Every girl hopes for it...their fairytale love. There isn't one girl out there that hasn't dreamt about meeting their soulmate...and here I've met mine at 25. Well. I met him at 23. *(She laughs.)* We didn't really meet in the most fairytale of ways... We both happened to be in this cafe, and it was really crowded. I was sitting with my friends, and he was walking behind me with his drink and...whoosh! He spilled hot coffee all down my back. Ruined my shirt and gave me third degree burns. I still have some of the scars. *(She laughs.)* It was worth it. I'd take burns over my whole body if it meant...that none of this has happened. *(She sighs.)* Those three years that we dated were next to perfect. We'd do the funnest things together. Bowling. Hiking. Picnics. Even simple movie nights were fun. I just loved being with him. Kaden would always come up with these cute little games for us to play. Like if we'd see each other somewhere unexpected, like the market, we'd act like we didn't know each other. And follow one another around and flirt like we were meeting for the first time. I didn't even care when he told me he was a recovering alcoholic. It didn't mean much to me, just that we wouldn't be going to any bars. I didn't...I don't understand how someone as perfect as my Kaden, my soulmate. Could be an addict. It just doesn't fit. Honestly, I hardly even think about the fact. Since I've never drank much it was easy to banish the stuff from my life to make his easier. When he proposed, under the stars over a homemade picnic on the roof of my apartment, it had crossed my mind that we couldn't have champagne at the wedding but... It doesn't make sense. My Kaden would never be an addict. Judi has to be right. He just drinks to appease Ethan. *(Her face darkens.)* Ethan's just a burden. A good for nothing drunk himself. During the past three years, all Kaden ever says that Ethan is doing is partying. He's the one that shoulda been in that ditch. I swear here and now if we...when we make it through this, Ethan will never be part of Kaden's life ever again. Ever.

*(**TEGAN** splashes her face once more then turns to exit.)*

Scene Seven

(TEGAN enters, much more composed, to see that the roles have changed and JUDI is now crying into ETHAN's shoulder. TEGAN glares and goes to sit the corner.)

ETHAN. Tegan, will you please get over here?

TEGAN. No.

ETHAN. Why not?

TEGAN. I have no desire to sit next to you.

ETHAN. Will you please stop being so stubborn? I don't care if you blame me or God or anyone else, but the three of us are in the same boat right now, and –

TEGAN. Oh. I blame you.

ETHAN. Whatever, Tea! Please just come over here.

(JUDI sits up and wipes her eyes nodding. The mother once more.)

JUDI. Yes. Tegan just come here. We have to support each other or we're not going to make it through this moment.

TEGAN. Support each other? Support each other?

(TEGAN stands and crosses to them as ETHAN stands. Her voice raising with each word.)

Were you supporting Kaden when you let him hang out with drunks in high school? Was Ethan supporting Kad when he took him that party and let him drink?

(The next few lines are spoken over each other:)

JUDI. Tegan!

ETHAN. You don't know what you're talking about.

TEGAN. Yes, I do Ethan!

(At this point ETHAN and TEGAN begin to yell at each other about whose fault it is. Laying the blame. Trying to explain their own reasoning. It should be fast paced and hard to understand.)

(**JUDI** *stands, but steps back from the two, her face a mask of shock. Stage right the* **DOCTOR** *and the* **NURSE** *enter, going unnoticed by the trio.*)

NURSE. Rockwell? Kaden Rockwell?

(They go on fighting, unnoticing, they are so caught up.)

DOCTOR. Is Kaden Rockwell's family here?

(The **DOCTOR***'s booming voice breaks through the fight ,and they go silent turning towards the* **DOCTOR***. Staring at him for a moment.* **JUDI** *is the first to recover. Rushing across the stage to them.* **ETHAN** *and* **TEGAN** *on her heels.)*

NURSE. Are you the Rockwells?

JUDI. Yes.

(pause)

JUDI, ETHAN, TEGAN. So?

(The **DOCTOR** *clears his throat and moves forward.)*

DOCTOR. So. I have some news.

The End

NAVY BLUE TILES

by Katarzyna Roszczeda

CHARACTER BREAKDOWN

SOPHIE DAVIS: She is all-American and in her late 20s. She wears a pink long sleeved sweater, blue jeans, a white apron that has the name of the bakery on it, and a thin pink headband. Her hair is pulled back into a ponytail. She is a quiet, "keep to herself" kind of person. She is also slightly sensitive and a perfectionist. Vincent is her ex-boyfriend.

VINCENT GIAMMANCO: He is Italian, tall, in his early 30s. He has short dark hair that is drenched in water. His clothes stick to his body making his lean muscles visible. He wears dark jeans, a dark red flannel that is unbuttoned, exposing a white shirt underneath, a leather jacket, and sneakers that make squeaky noises when he walks. He is a player, the "big man on campus." He knows he is good looking, which makes him cocky.

PETER O'CONNOLEY SMITH: He is British. He is a doctor in his early 30s. He is compassionate and enjoys helping others. He is Sophie's friend.

ABOUT THE PLAYWRIGHT

Katarzyna Roszczeda was born in New York but raised in Poland. She was seventeen when her piece, *Navy Blue Tiles*, was published. She hopes to continue writing in the future.

(Lights up. It is evening in late December in the present day. It is pouring outside. Thunder can be heard from time to time and lightning flashes. "Sugar Baby's Bakery" is elaborately decorated for the holidays. Christmas carol music, is heard softly in the background. The aroma of cookies, cakes, and cupcakes fills the air. The bakery, located in Williamsburg, Brooklyn, has several small intricate white tables and matching chairs. On stage right, there is a display case of the sugary treats stored inside. A mistletoe hangs by the door on stage left.)

*(**SOPHIE DAVIS** is center stage, cleaning the surface of the tables as she is preparing to close up. She glances swiftly at the clock hanging on the wall by the cashier, behind the display case. She walks behind the counter and quickly cleans the case with a cloth and Windex. When she is finished, she wipes her hands on her apron and takes a bite out of the yellow cupcake that had been carefully placed on the stack of other cupcakes. Enter* **VINCENT GIAMMANCO**.*)*

SOPHIE. *(doesn't look up and speaks over her shoulder)* Sorry, we're closed.

VINCENT. Well, according to this sign on the door, you're not.

SOPHIE. *(walks over to the door and flips the sign on the other side so that it reads "Closed")* There. Now you can leave.

*(**SOPHIE** returns to the counter, takes the cupcake she began eating and sits at one of the tables.)*

VINCENT. *(dramatizing and placing his hand over his heart)* Ouch. That's gonna leave a mark.

(Smiling, he makes his way towards her, attempting to hug her.)

SOPHIE. *(stands up and takes a step back, defensively)* Listen fella, if you don't leave now, I'll call the cops.

(She takes out her cell phone from her apron to prove it and speaks in a threatening tone.)

I have them on speed dial.

VINCENT. *(disregarding tone.)* Wow, Sophie. I can't believe you still say that.

SOPHIE. *(stunned that he knows her name.)* Wait.

(Pause as a realization occurs. Takes a step forward.)

Vince? Is that you?

VINCENT. Yeah…Who else did you think it was?

SOPHIE. *(running to him and hugging him)* Oh my God! Vince! I can't believe it! You're back!

VINCENT. *(laughing)* I can't believe you still work here. How do you make business when you scare all the customers with your nasty attitude?

SOPHIE. *(with attitude)* What attitude?

*(They laugh. **SOPHIE** leads **VINCENT** to a table at centerstage. He takes off his jacket, hangs it on the back of his chair, and they sit down.)*

VINCENT. So I hear that you run this place now.

SOPHIE. I've been running it for five years.

VINCENT. *(looking around)* And you've changed everything! I swear there used to be white, blue and green tiles on the floor.

SOPHIE. *(irritated)* They weren't blue. They were navy.

VINCENT. *(with a wave of his hand)* Same difference.

SOPHIE. *(shaking her head)* No, it's not the same. I thought we had settled this already.

VINCENT. *(sitting back, with arms crossed)* Then I guess we didn't.

SOPHIE. Well, apparently you haven't changed. I don't know how I could have gone along with you when you were this stubborn.

VINCENT. I was stubborn?! Look at you!

SOPHIE. I can't believe you're insulting me in my bakery.

VINCENT. You think someone's going to take you seriously when you named your bakery "Sugar Baby?"

SOPHIE. You think someone's going to take YOU seriously when you tell them you love 'em then you decide to run off to the military? *(a moment's silence)* Look, I'm sorry. It was in the heat of the moment and...I didn't mean–

VINCENT. *(seriously)* No. You're absolutely right. We can't avoid the subject forever. We might as well let it out in the open so that we can move past it and forgive each other.

SOPHIE. *(walking to the counter to put away the cloth and Windex)* Oh, there's no need for that. Believe me, I have moved on.

VINCENT. *(following **SOPHIE**)* Oh, come on, Sophie! We were in a serious relationship and I–

SOPHIE. I get it, okay? I'm not mad at you.

VINCENT. Just listen to me–

SOPHIE. *(takes the Windex and cloth out again)* I don't need to.

VINCENT. Sophie, what are you doing?

SOPHIE. *(spraying Windex all over the counter)* I missed a spot.

(He takes the Windex and cloth out of her hands and puts them aside. He turns her around so that she is facing him. His arms are around her.)

VINCENT. Sophie, please, don't be like this.

SOPHIE. *(defensively)* Like what?

VINCENT. The way you are now.

SOPHIE. *(snappy)* Well, I'm sorry if that bothers you.

VINCENT. *(angry)* Stop making it sound as if it was my fault.

SOPHIE. Then whose is it? *Mine?*

VINCENT. *(apologetically)* No, of course not...but do you honestly think I wanted to leave you?

SOPHIE. *(Crosses center stage. Dryly)* I don't know what to think anymore.

VINCENT. Sophie, when I signed up, I thought it was for the training. You know the navy gives you a full scholarship for college *and* it looks really good on your resume.

SOPHIE. *(mocking)* So are you in Harvard now?

VINCENT. No, I got rejected. **(SOPHIE** *smirks.)* What? Do I look like a fortune teller to you? Bam! It's 9/11. I had no idea I was gonna be shipped off to Afghanistan.

SOPHIE. Yeah, go ahead, blame the terrorists for your stupidity.

VINCENT. *(proudly)* You know, I served my country.

SOPHIE. *(sarcastically)* Did you win any medals?

VINCENT. Why are you so mad at me for this? It's not as if I didn't write to you. I thought about you every second I was there.

SOPHIE. Really? Every second?

VINCENT. Okay, so maybe not *every* second, but most of the time. And when I thought about you, I started thinking about us. I thought about what I would say to you when I first saw you. Man, do you know how many different ways you can say the word "hi"?

SOPHIE. I guess I never let you reenact that?

VINCENT. No you didn't. And when I came here, I was still expecting to see the diner: the worn out couches, the tiny graffiti mark someone made at the end of the table that used to be right…. *(He twirls his finger midair and points to the left of center stage)* there, and our white, blue, and green tiles. *(looking around)* But I wasn't expecting THIS. I don't like what you've done with this place. Not one bit. It was in the *diner* that I met you. It was in the *diner* that we had our first kiss. It was in the *diner* that I told you I loved you. And now… it's as if that place doesn't exist anymore, like it never existed.

SOPHIE. *(quietly mimicking him)* It was also in the *diner* that you told me you're leaving.

VINCENT. *(shocked for a moment then whispering tenderly)* Sophie. I'm so sorry.

*(He pulls her in a tight hug. At first, **SOPHIE** does not hug him back, but then she embraces him. At that moment, **VINCENT** pulls away quickly and moves behind the counter, not taking his eyes off the floor.)*

What's this?

SOPHIE. What's what?

VINCENT. *(shocked)* There's a blue tile.

SOPHIE. Navy.

VINCENT. You left a blue tile.

SOPHIE. I said it's navy.

VINCENT. *(excited)* I can't believe it! Sophie! Why didn't you tell me?

SOPHIE. I did! I told you, it's navy. The reconstruction cost a lot and –

VINCENT. Oh Sophie, stop making excuses. Just tell me you still love me.

SOPHIE. *(walking towards the door)* No. If I'd say that I'd be lying. I told you before. I've moved on. I think it'd be best if you leav–

*(She reaches for the door, but **VINCENT**, who has been following her, pushes the door, closing it as **SOPHIE** turns around. One hand is up, leaning on the door, and the other is lingering on her waist. They are really close. **VINCENT** is enjoying this; **SOPHIE** is a bit nervous.)*

VINCENT. *(playfully)* I'm supposed to believe you've moved on?

SOPHIE. Y-yes.

VINCENT. *(laughing)* Sophie, you were always a bad liar.

SOPHIE. *(annoyed now)* You know what, believe what you want. I don't care anymore.

VINCENT. See? You can't even make something up!

SOPHIE. *(pissed off)* I don't need to make anything up. *(quickly)* I have a fiancé.

VINCENT. *(unconvinced)* Do you?

SOPHIE. As a matter of fact, I do. His name's Peter O'Connoley Smith.

VINCENT. Is it?

SOPHIE. Yes. His hair's black and he has brown eyes. *(proudly)* He's a doctor.

VINCENT. *(laughing)* Uh huh.

SOPHIE. While *you* were off killing people, *he* devoted his time and money searching for a cure to cancer.

VINCENT. And let me guess, he didn't succeed.

SOPHIE. Oh, well, he didn't give up yet. *(changing the subject)* Did I tell you that he's very intelligent? And he loves children.

VINCENT. *(astonished)* When did I tell you I don't love children?

SOPHIE. *(snappy)* Stop making everything about you!

VINCENT. Okay, so he's tall, dark, and handsome. I get the picture.

SOPHIE. No, you don't. He's a lean, mean, money-making machine.

VINCENT. So you're dating him for his money?

SOPHIE. I'm not dating him. *(stretching the word "engaged")* We're *engaged*. And the money's just a bonus.

VINCENT. Then where's your engagement ring?

(**SOPHIE** *looks down at her finger which holds no ring. When she looks back up,* **VINCENT** *kisses her.*)

SOPHIE. *(pushing him away)* Why'd you do that?

VINCENT. First of all, I'm in love with you. That should be reason enough, but F.Y.I., we're standing under the mistletoe. I was under obligation.

SOPHIE. No. I put it up for my f–

VINCENT. Yeah, yeah, yeah…you and your imaginary "fiancé." The way I see it, it was you who came to the door knowing that the mistletoe was there. Then, you could have just walked away before I even kissed you.

*(Enter **PETER** from the kitchen. He is drying his hands on a small towel. **VINCENT** is shocked to see him. **SOPHIE** is looking down at the floor.)*

PETER. Well, good news. The loo is up and running.

*(**PETER** goes over to **SOPHIE** and kisses her on the cheek. Speaks to **VINCENT**)*

Oh, hello there, mate. The name's Peter.

*(Offers to shake hands with **VINCENT**, but **VINCENT** just stares at him.)*

Are you alright, mate?

*(**PETER** turns his attention to **SOPHIE**.)*

Is he alright?

SOPHIE. He'll be fine.

PETER. Okay, well, in that case, I better be leaving. The hospital called. Someone canceled and my shift begins in an hour –

SOPHIE. So you can't make it to the restaurant for dinner tonight.

PETER. Basically. I'll make it up to you. I promise.

*(**PETER** kisses **SOPHIE** on the cheek.)*

SOPHIE. Okay.

PETER. Cheerio!

*(Exit **PETER**.)*

VINCENT. I'm guessing that's Peter.

SOPHIE. Let me explain.

VINCENT. You don't have to.

SOPHIE. Yes, I do. First of all, I walked over here to open you the door. So you can leave. Don't get too carried away with your fantasies about me. Secondly, I'm stuck. I tied my apron and it must have gotten lodged when you slammed the door shut. See? I can't move.

(She indicates. **VINCENT** *moves around her to open the door, thus, freeing her.)*

VINCENT. *(starts exiting, then pauses, not turning around to face* **SOPHIE.***)* So the blue tile meant nothing?

SOPHIE. The *navy* tile meant nothing.

*(***VINCENT** *nods. He exits, disappointed.* **SOPHIE** *walks behind the counter slowly and stares at the navy tile. She looks around the bakery and notices* **VINCENT**'s *leather jacket resting on a chair. She walks over to it, and picks it up, glancing it over. Then, she puts it on, snuggling into it, and zipping it up. All this time, she has her back to the door and, therefore, does not notice* **VINCENT**'s *re-entrance. At first,* **VINCENT** *it shocked. Then, he leans against a chair by the door, and watches* **SOPHIE** *with a slight smirk on his lips.)*

VINCENT. It looks good on you.

*(***SOPHIE** *jumps, startled.)*

SOPHIE. *(nervously)* I thought you had left.

VINCENT. *(pointing)* I forgot my jacket.

SOPHIE. Right.

(She removes the jacket and hands it to **VINCENT**. *During the exchange, their hands touch and none of them pulls away. They gaze into each others' eyes.)*

VINCENT. Okay, so...I better get going.

(He turns towards the door, then changes his mind and turns around, facing **SOPHIE.***)*

I don't understand you.

SOPHIE. What's there to understand?

VINCENT. Why were you trying on my jacket?

SOPHIE. I like the design.

VINCENT. Or do you like the person it belongs to?

SOPHIE. Weren't you about to leave?

VINCENT. Aren't you getting married?

SOPHIE. It's just a jacket –

VINCENT. And it doesn't mean anything. You know, you say that a lot.

SOPHIE. Say what?

VINCENT. "It doesn't mean anything." Just like you said with the blue tile.

SOPHIE. Navy.

VINCENT. Whatever. But I think it means something.

SOPHIE. You're going crazy again.

VINCENT. Am I? Or am I hitting the bulls-eye?

SOPHIE. You don't even know what you're saying.

VINCENT. But you do.

SOPHIE. *(turning away)* I don't want to argue with you again.

VINCENT. We're not arguing.

SOPHIE. *(turning back to him)* Then what is this?

VINCENT. Talking.

SOPHIE. *(to herself)* How can anyone stand you?

VINCENT. What was that?

SOPHIE. Are you going to leave or should I?

VINCENT. Wow…there's so much anger coming from you.

SOPHIE. How do you do this?

VINCENT. Do what?

SOPHIE. You always find a new way to piss me off.

VINCENT. I really don't understand you.

SOPHIE. What, are we gonna start this conversation all over again?

VINCENT. Why do you have trouble admitting your feelings?

SOPHIE. What feelings?

VINCENT. Well there's no use denying them.

SOPHIE. What do you want me to say? Yes, I'm still in love with you! Are you happy now? Are you satisfied? There! You got what you want.

VINCENT. *(teasing)* So you admit, after all this time, that you still love me?

SOPHIE. Yes, you moron! I still love you! But you didn't even realize how much it hurt me when you left. You just packed your things and POOF! You were gone. And you know what? You want to know what I think? You're pathetic. You had everything here. You had me! And you still left. But you know what? When I realized it was you who came into my bakery, I wanted to prove that I was just fine without you. That I didn't need you. That you were just a faint memory from my past. That I didn't love you. I wanted you to see what a glorious life I am living. I run my own bakery and I'm engaged to a doctor. I wanted you to be jealous of me. I wanted you to see what you lost. I wanted you to see just how *stupid* you were. So you coming back here, I wanted you to know one thing. I'm not going to be easily won over. I'm not going to run into your arms and confess my love for you like in some of those cheesy romantic comedy movies.

You shouldn't have expected me to sit around here waiting for you to return because that is just plain silly. Yes, I think about you constantly. I imagine us together, but then I replay the memory of the day you left. And all that love for you makes soooo me angry. *(taking a breath)* I guess I'm more pathetic than you.

VINCENT. Wow. That's the longest speech I have ever heard you say.

SOPHIE. *(sitting down, tired of arguing)* Forget it Vince. Forget everything I said. Obviously, it means nothing to you.

VINCENT. Nothing to me? Do you know what you just put me through? *(mimicking her)* "I don't love you, Vince! Yes, I love you. I don't love you anymore. But I still have feelings for you. You're a moron! I keep thinking about you. You're pathetic Vince!" Ahhhhhhhhhhhh-hhhh! Stick to one story, damn it!

SOPHIE. *(defensively)* I didn't put you through all that –

VINCENT. Wait a minute. You still love me?

SOPHIE. Are you stupid?

VINCENT. Then, who's Peter Pan?

SOPHIE. Peter who?

VINCENT. *(shocked)* You forgot about your fiancé? Wait. Does that me you're cheating on him with me?

SOPHIE. I'm not cheating on him and I'm not with you.

VINCENT. *(twitching his eyebrows up and down and smiling)* Oh, I get it. You want to keep this a secret.

SOPHIE. What secret?! We're not together.

VINCENT. *(confused)* I thought you said you still loved me.

SOPHIE. I do.

VINCENT. Sophie, you are seriously giving me mixed signals here. You love me and I love you. That makes us lovers. So, technically, you're cheating.

SOPHIE. Did you not pay any attention to what I said before?

VINCENT. I got the gist of it.

SOPHIE. Then what do you want?

(Lights out. Thunder can be heard louder than before.)

VINCENT. What just happened?

SOPHIE. The lights went out.

VINCENT. Okay, I'm coming to you. *(He attempts to walk to Sophie, banging into chairs on the way, making them fall.)*

SOPHIE. Wait there. I'll get my flashlight.

(She takes out her cell phone, and using the light from it, she walks behind the counter. She finds the flashlight and turns it on. She walks to Vincent.)

VINCENT. Well your British doctor boyfriend fixed the "loo", does he know how to fix the lights?

SOPHIE. He's not-

*(Banging on the door. **SOPHIE** and **VINCENT** jump, startled.)*

VINCENT. *(Shielding her with his arm)* Whatever it is, I'll protect you.

(**SOPHIE** *rolls her eyes and approaches the door, with* **VINCENT** *at her heels.* **SOPHIE** *flashes the flashlight at the door.* **PETER** *is there.* **SOPHIE** *crosses to open the door for him, but* **VINCENT** *stops her.*)

SOPHIE. What are you doing?

VINCENT. We are not letting him in.

SOPHIE. Are you insane?

VINCENT. Why on earth would I let my arch-enemy in here?

SOPHIE. It's raining!

VINCENT. He can deal with it.

SOPHIE. You're acting like a baby right now.

VINCENT. I'm not going to stay in the same room with him.

SOPHIE. You won't have to. He'll be here with me and you can stay in the bathroom.

VINCENT. You're cruel. *(pause)* Actually, come to think of it, I have a few words to say to Pete.

SOPHIE. It's Peter.

VINCENT. Same thing. I guess it has come to this. I'll do whatever I have to to win you over.

(Vincent rolls up his sleeves, cracks his knuckles, and turns his head from side to side, preparing to fight.)

Okay, I'm ready. I'm lettin him in.

SOPHIE. *(Trying to stop him)* Vincent, it's not what you think.

VINCENT. Don't worry about me, Sophie, I'll be fine. I can take him. *(He opens the door, ignoring* **SOPHIE**'*s protests, then quickly closes it.)* By any chance, does he know karate, martial arts or wrestling or anything like that?

SOPHIE. No, he's against violence.

VINCENT. *(Smiling)* Good. *(He opens the door again, letting* **PETER** *inside.* **PETER** *is drenched.)*

PETER. It's about time you let me in.

VINCENT. *(Blocking* **PETER**'*s path)* It's about time we settled this.

SOPHIE. Vince, stop!

VINCENT. Don't pity him, Sophie. He chose his own fate. *(He's about to punch Peter.)*

SOPHIE. He's my step brother!

VINCENT. *(Stunned)* Say that again?

SOPHIE. I made everything up.

VINCENT. *(To* **PETER** *in British slang and nodding his head in her direction)* You don't fancy her?

PETER. *(Shocked)* Jeez! You're a madman!

VINCENT. *(Nervous smile)* Well then. That's settled. Sorry about that, it was a misunderstanding. Wasn't it Sophie? Let's just forget about this and ...

PETER. Forget about this? I was two seconds away from a nose job. And for what reason? What have I possibly done to you? For God's sake, you don't even know me! *(To* **SOPHIE***)* After all these years that you've been blabbing about Vincent this and Vincent that, I thought he must have been something great.

VINCENT. *(To* **SOPHIE***)* Ahh ... so apparently you've been blabbing about me?

PETER. Oh please. *(Walks to the tile)* Do you see this tile? I told her to take it out when we were remodeling this place, but she insisted upon keeping it there. Now in my opinion, it just makes this bakery look mismatched. But Sophie said that there are a lot of memories packed into this little square. Your memories. *(Approaching them)* So now, would you quit arguing? You're both still in love with each other so what's this banter all about? Any idiot can sense the level of tension in this room. Now Sophie, I've been there every step of the way for you, from getting this business up and running to unsuccessfully helping you move on. But you'll have to take it from here. *(About to exit)* Oh and Vincent? *(Removing a badge from his jacket)* I work part time with the NYPD. Be careful who you pick a fight with.

VINCENT. *(Stunned)* Good to know. *(***PETER** *exits.* **VINCENT** *and* **SOPHIE** *sit. Lights on.)*

SOPHIE. So where do we go from here?

VINCENT. What can I say, the blue tile gives me some hope.
SOPHIE. It's navy. And I'm surprised you still have hope.
VINCENT. No, Sophie, it's blue. Stop being such a pessimist.
SOPHIE. It's navy, and I'm not a pessimist.
VINCENT. It's BLUE.
SOPHIE. NA-VY.
VINCENT. *(stretching the word out)* BL-UE.
SOPHIE. I think I know what color it is if I was staring at it for five years!
VINCENT. I think I know what color it is if I was standing right on it!
SOPHIE. Well, maybe you can't see the color because your giant feet were covering it up!
VINCENT. What are you talking about? My feet aren't that big.
SOPHIE. Weren't you apologizing just a few minutes ago?
VINCENT. *(putting his hands up defensively)* How about we start all over? *(He walks over to the door. Reenacting)* Hey Sophie, you look great! *(She stands. They walk to each other and embrace as the lights fade.)*

www.ingramcontent.com/pod-product-compliance
Lightning Source LLC
Chambersburg PA
CBHW071840290426
44109CB00017B/1888